IN PRAISE OF THE HEALER

Swallow the word.

Swallow the tongue.

                              Swallow down

                    the fullness in the throat.

FARTHER / FATHER

Our dead call out our dead / *you show your filthy face*

You useless tit / you runt / you piece of shit / a shame

Unleashed by plain-talk / begging before a threshing

From the old butcher / your leather strap / unbelted

Crescent buckle for a skinning / hiding / each of us /

Slickened with blood / held down in your hinterland

Each barren mile unabating / *say mercy.*

What dwells in the dog's sleep / unbounded / darkness

The closer you are to the sun the more difficult you are

To see / penumbral / who runs from whom / until kept

Down / cowering / I do not move / you will not move.

You are no less dangerous than you were as you drag

Your bones / field stones / we never once wept upon

The firmament / eight children left with the lone wife

Who would not carry the quiet / the final cardiac pall

Paled thirty years / crescent moons / scars strapped

Below the heart.

A finisher with a surly disposition / *better run boy*

Run / before the shadow on an August day / flight

Of the dove interrupted / who should feel shame /

Worthless idlers / caught neurotic / we are taught

You will not be tamed.

Dirige / *domine* / *deus meus* / ignominious father / aberration

Uttered solemn / all you missed is nothing / *noli me tangere* /

Don't touch me.

Each child dragged by its hair across the linoleum /

Given lip / *good for nothing* / illicit / dust / dusk-lit

Let these bygones / cease holding on to me.

We brace in the centre / attention / nothing more than this

Far-fetched ruckus / rot-gut fuss / a latched door farmhouse

Taunting / the slap-board remains / rants / lashed feverish

Your day's demands / fraught / cling to the bleak / this filth

In plain sight / *I am a man possessed.*

Beyond two graves / yours and the child's / a sole

Pine fallen from a lack of forest / the sun-downed

Dove-wing unfolds / under night / your closeness

Lies too close.

Birch box and iron nails / buried under the cover of lichen

Scrolled years / each letter etched by lime / faded shame

Be a lesser phantom / of the bleak / you will receive no less

No blossom braided in the child's hair.

Rosemarie / rose of thorn / rose up from prairie

Wherever you have gone you will not take her /

Unfollowed to a harrow / kin / stone / infanta

Sub rosa / only her eyes cry.

Our dire wolf / bewildered / breath taken in plain sight /

Before the sun is farthest south / ruck-sacked / a shadow

Across the face / red zenith / dog-light / *Dead Dog Creek*

In the faithful hour / his small body filled with buckshot

Carry him / carry him.

Undreamt / the sleeper remains untouched.

I've been meaning to say / I belly-ache / *useless tit*

Found the rain barrel with our long-drowned dove.

After the diminishing / dirt body kicked against kitchen wall /

Kept alive / what mercy has lessened / quietened as we speak

Of light / spoiled / *cry-babying* / a bunkum transubstantiated

Our cunning remains within.

Any radiance seen is due to perspective / at the first ascension

Night cold will come as reprieve / as rescue / we sad animals

All of us wet behind the ears / we still drag our own wet skins.

Even death is a quiet / even the fiercest sleep / after another day

An hour bent to water / a catch-song shudders from the diviner /

A bough cut for the wellspring.

Unearthing the horizon / uncertain if the sun is low / west

Or rising east / luminous / hourglass tipped to the wheat /

Ghosts / our harvest sheen.

Holder of the dog's bones / night-fallen creek / current home

Borne back / broken / the limp body / still writhing / we will

Never depend upon our eyes.

Submerged / without air / within water / us / small-sacked

In the last hour / the equinox / relinquished / moonward

Out of my sight / a wife's tale / we find you not as we want

You / still where you are / dead on the floor / facing down

The long shadow / incalculable / we await the whimper

Eyes lowering / descent of the casket / no axis spinning /

Stars dying / *no* / they are already gone.

IN PRAISE OF THE HEALER

Eclipse the eye of the dark.

Open the mouth.

Breathe you in.

Hold the breath.

CLASP

You and I—confined to our scrying room. Every falter of the limbs and every muscle of the face exposed to view. You are what I am. You cause as much sorrow. In what worse way could we vent this rage than by beating this head against these walls?

Sing for me. You seized the words out of my mouth—who suffers the most? You keep it all in. Noise—no noise. You upset me, *baby*. And you can't do that.

We're never left alone. Consider what the means are—we can't lose what we haven't ever had. You asked for it. You won't get mercy. You are no more a whisper.

Sleep is for the weak.

I collected the reasons against it, which were in every body's mouth.
I marked them down, with, I think, some additions. (You may or may not
remember.)

I feign now pleasure—sleep in splendour—notwithstanding
the sadness of the subject.

(Please read the letter.)

A fool could read the signs.

The point then, settled. I can't keep it in, can't do it anymore. What then, you will say—I can't. Perhaps—I can't be alone, I can't be with you, can't stop. And for my own part, I have no fear of it.

I can't explain—others perhaps might. And yet, I can't forget, especially when there is nothing to be lost by it. I assure you, I can't help myself. I can't breathe.

IN PRAISE OF THE HEALER

After the long sought

reckon—

surrender.

Say, *with my body I thee worship*.

VIGIL / VESTIGE

The riven escapes—
distorts
into the fierce and monstrous
unless encountered
as a lover
held
closely.

After the revering—
a vestige—
we
of one
of two.

Decide what to keep.

Acushla
darkling—
sleight body marked by sighing.

Agonal
half-breath
on the verge of quiet.

Purblind the breeze—
we belong to grey hours
breaking.

The first time we are awake.

We left
believing our demons
with their sepulchral dreams sing false
and without
meaning.

                    Carved
openings for them to crawl back into—
as if they could
now
more dead than they were
from our grieving.

Eye-shine—
you of the equinox, unequivocal
and left forgone.

Be still
love—

creatio ex nihilo.

Ecstatic
and prone to rapture
in the hours before dawn.

Beckoned to the lake—
to the ruin.

The scripture of leaves.

Our salvage—
shivering by the weeds.

We falter toward the good—
for the smallest amount of the most worthless thing.

Sleepless
with shy sweats
and the cold we're night-blind by.

Our after-dream terrors
of a slaughterhouse—
or a labyrinth
akin
to a slaughterhouse.

Stone omen—
scabrous to the touch
and bruising.

Auspicious as a scapegrace—
dissipating
another's trouble.

A malediction moaned
through clenched teeth.

All is for the best.

Baleful
our mouths fill
before the mutable—
surrendered to the sun-lapse.

We murmur for sleep after slaughter—
and would drink from any
ruined
pool.

A shadow-fall—
after the half-clasp
relinquished to the late blazon.

We are not beautiful but beautifully inspired—
and left with less.

Amo. Amas. Amat.

We ghost-slip out from the drowning.

Silvering—a shudder from the deep
up to the shore—

We let our dead climb on top of us.

This is the first time we are awake.

Even our bodies suffer their own love.

As blood, as water—
drawn out after days.

Amamus. Amatis. Amant.

Press deep and rest in me—
there is space enough for us both to die.

IN PRAISE OF THE HEALER

Of course

the inevitable

rupture in my chest

from the heart's opening.

Courage—

stay in my arms

until

you can't.

DIRGE

We fail to name this right / without the words

For lapsing / lilies / wilted / in the beginning

Wind caught nothing / your leaf unscrawled.

Whatever we've come to collect / we can't find

The undaunted / spectral / *let's put it this way*

Transverse / the waves lengthen ungraspable

Umbral / fear departing as soon as it's spoken

We turned toward your haunting / a sallowed

Rustle / rustle.

Slender and tenuous in the eventual

Velvet quell / weak pulse / (no echo)

Silenced / narrow your eyes to now.

De novo / the star-burst cell / swelling in

Beneath a meniscus / spectrum / spread

Unbounded / the mind's eye dilated blue

A lake turned over / in the hastened light

The noumenal / final refusal / held back.

Can you feel my hand? / here is your hand.

Conspectus tuo viam meam / direct a way

With your sight.

Out of a glimpse / the storm-fold / veer toward

A last evening / unrivalled defiance / *vaporum*

Vaporum / unravelled / plainsong / swift bled

From your Sylvian scar.

Of course I feel dead inside.

Of course you knew that was coming.

After the slide of a blade / the slight / sheened

(You may linger like this for some time.)

Word-blind / shift aphasic / *what I mean is no*

And no and no and no and no /

(Wakeful bareness) / we've seen you of this place

As the raw-such / denial / undiscerned as an echo

Unsought and left behind / the ghosted / skyward

As the essential / sylph / shadow / detached from

A great shade / shale eyes / released to darkening

Night / only you are present when the heart stops.

If you can't speak / write in a fissured / alter-language

Of nerve-matter / *dura mater* / orbit of the central axis

By a crevice / scattered / *venous lacunae* / lamina code

Cambered whisp to a fold / a tremor / (footfall) / rustle

Shudder leaves / whelming the surface / sleep / *no* and

No / resumed in doubling / parietal / occipital / *rostrum*

And *sulcus* / unsettled / perceptible at the cleft / curved

Lobes and tracts / gestures exhausted / serene.

These are your August blackberries / this is my hand.

Ash to water / to earth / stone turns / urn to ground.

Apportion the indivisible / out of dust / bone

From the lifted hold-all / dead-weight settled

To the bottom / your whole / unbearably light.

Four hands and your spade / forcing the severed

Roots / bare earth's upheaval / oathing / opening

Downturned / downward / your burying spade.

That which would not be buried

Floated on the water / what part

Of your body / all of your body

Water-body in our wine glass.

Pact-sent / soothe-seekers / after a fading vigil

As body-bearers / ash-tenders / mouths open

For air / in water / an elemental lull / till wet

Transmutes to quicksilver as you head under

This cusp of autumn / dive to the cold.

Let's put it this way / *forgive each occlusion*

In my mind / rain-worn worry / run-down

To a lake / ineluctable / window / curtain

Your eyes / close / *stop.*

Do you understand?

Do I understand?

Are you laughing now?

Weeping.

Do you understand?

I understand.

This is difficult for you to say.

This is difficult for you to say.

IN PRAISE OF THE HEALER

Wet by the shallows—our willow.

You do not cry because you cannot. I will not cry because you do not.

You give my hands the weight of your body.

Rest in me.

What I mean is this is where I choose to die.

NOTES / ACKNOWLEDGMENTS

An excerpt of 'In Praise of the Healer' was included in Chris Turnbull's 2013 FootPress Project: 'Rout/e,' and can be found, waiting out the seasons, in the form of trail markers through a grove of black walnut trees in Kemptville, Ontario.

'Farther / Father' received third prize for the 2015 Banff Centre Bliss Carman Poetry Award and was published in *Prairie Fire*.

'Clasp' is a response to Michèle Provost's 'Playlist,' a multiform art installation exhibited at Ottawa's Dale Smith Gallery in 2011. The poem was written, in part, with Jeremy Bentham's Panopticon in mind. Originally a longer polyvocal piece, it was performed by Christine McNair, Sean Moreland, Glenn Nuotio, Carmel Purkis, Grant Wilkins, and me at Gallery 101 and at the National Art Centre's Fourth Stage. An audio-poem of one section can be found at *ourteeth.wordpress.com;* an excerpt was also published by *newpoerty.ca*

An early version of 'Vigil / Vestige' was commissioned by rob mclennan and Ottawa's Redwall Gallery as an engagement with Pedro Isztin's photo installation, 'Study of Structure and Form'. One excerpt became a video-poem and a broadside created in association with the Toronto Poetry Vendors in 2012; other excerpts were published in *Touch the Donkey, Concrete & River,* and *Matrix Magazine*.

'Dirge' was published in the second issue of *Canthius* in 2016.

My thanks to the City of Ottawa and the Ontario Arts Council for funding received, and for their continued, sustaining support of the arts.

Gratitude to co-conspirators, creators, curators, and friends: Silvija Barons, Jason Christie, Elisabeth de Mariaffi, Amanda Earl, kevin mcpherson eckhoff, Claire Farley, Susan Gillis, Steven Heighton, Pedro Isztin, Jennifer Londry, John W. MacDonald, rob mclennan, Christine McNair, Max Middle, Sean Moreland, George Murray, Glenn Nuotio, Pearl Pirie, Michèle Provost, Carmel Purkis, Peter Richardson, Su Rogers, Eric Slankis, Jennifer Still, Chris Turnbull, Grant Wilkins, and to the BookThug corps: Jay MillAr, Hazel Millar, Ruth Zuchter, Kate Hargreaves, and Phil Hall.

Multiple-award-winning poet, instructor, and editor Sandra Ridley is the author of three books of poetry: *Fallout* (winner of a 2010 Saskatchewan Book Award and the Alfred G. Bailey Prize); *Post-Apothecary* (finalist for the ReLit and Archibald Lampman Awards); and *The Counting House* (published by BookThug in 2013; finalist for the Archibald Lampman Award and chosen as one of the top five poetry books of 2013 in *Quill & Quire*'s Readers' Poll). In 2015, Ridley was a finalist for the KM Hunter Artist Award for Literature. She lives in Ottawa.

Manufactured as the First Edition of *Silvija*
in the Fall of 2016 by BookThug.

Distributed in Canada by the Literary Press Group:
www.lpg.ca

Distributed in the US by Small Press Distribution:
www.spdbooks.org

Shop online at www.bookthug.ca

BOOK
PRODUCTION
WAR ECONOMY
STANDARD

Edited for the press by Phil Hall
Type + design by Kate Hargreaves
Copy edited by Ruth Zuchter